Bunnies

Kelly Doudna

Published by SandCastle™, an imprint of ABDO Publishing Company, 4940 Viking Drive, Edina, Minnesota 55435.

Printed in the United States.

Photo credits: Peter Arnold, Ian Beames/Ecoscene/Corbis, Arvind Garg/Corbis, Eric and David Hosking/Corbis, Philip Marazzi/Papilio/Corbis, Robert Pickett/Corbis, Michael Pole/Corbis, Annie Poole/Papilio/Corbis, Corel, Digital Stock, Kelly Doudna

Library of Congress Cataloging-in-Publication Data

Doudna, Kelly, 1963-
    Bunnies / Kelly Doudna.
       p. cm. -- (Baby animals)
    Summary: Describes the physical characteristics and behavior of young rabbits.
    ISBN 1-57765-184-7
    1. Rabbits--Infancy--Juvenile literature. [1. Rabbits--Infancy.
2. Animals--Infancy.] I. Title. II. Series: Doudna, Kelly, 1963-
Baby animals.
QL737.L32D68   1999
599.32'139--dc21

                                                    98-28346
                                                   CIP
                                                     AC

The SandCastle concept, content, and reading method have been reviewed and approved by a national advisory board including literacy specialists, librarians, elementary school teachers, early childhood education professionals, and parents.

Let Us Know

After reading the book, SandCastle would like you to tell us your stories about reading. What is your favorite page? Was there something hard that you needed help with? Share the ups and downs of learning to read. We want to hear from you! To get posted on the Abdo Publishing Company Web site, send us email at:

sandcastle@abdopub.com

SandCastle Level: Beginning

About SandCastle™

A professional team of educators, reading specialists, and content developers created the SandCastle™ series to support young readers as they develop reading skills and strategies and increase their general knowledge. The SandCastle™ series has four levels that correspond to early literacy development in young children. The levels are provided to help teachers and parents select the appropriate books for young readers.

Emerging Readers
(no flags)

Beginning Readers
(1 flag)

Transitional Readers
(2 flags)

Fluent Readers
(3 flags)

These levels are meant only as a guide. All levels are subject to change.

To see a complete list of SandCastle™ books and other nonfiction titles from ABDO Publishing Company, visit **www.abdopub.com** or contact us at:
4940 Viking Drive, Edina, Minnesota 55435 • 1-800-800-1312 • fax: 1-952-831-1632

A young rabbit is
a bunny.

Bunnies are small.

This bunny is brown.

It lives outside.

Some bunnies are
hard to see.

This bunny hides
in the tall grass.

This bunny needs
milk to grow.

This bunny lives
in the house.

15

This bunny sits
alone in the grass.

It is fun to pet a
soft bunny.

Some bunnies are
not really bunnies
at all!

Words I Can Read

Nouns

A noun is a person, place, or thing

bunny (BUHN-ee)
pp. 5, 7, 11, 13, 15, 17, 19
grass (GRASS) pp. 11, 17
house (HOWSS) p. 15
milk (MILK) p. 13
rabbit (RAB-it) p. 5

Plural Nouns

A plural noun is more than one
person, place, or thing

bunnies (BUHN-eez) pp. 5, 9, 21

Verbs

A verb is an action or being word

are (AR) pp. 5, 9, 21
grow (GROH) p. 13
hides (HYDZ) p. 11
is (IZ) pp. 5, 7, 19

lives (LIVZ) pp. 7, 15
needs (NEEDS) p. 13
pet (PET) p. 19
see (SEE) p. 9
sits (SITSS) p. 17

Adjectives

An adjective describes something

brown (BROWN) p. 7
fun (FUHN) p. 19
hard (HARD) p. 9
small (SMAWL) p. 5
soft (SAWFT) p. 19
some (SUHM) pp. 9, 21
tall (TAWL) p. 11
young (YUHNG) p. 5

Sight Words

grass

milk

house